Oxford International English

Emma Danihel

4

Workbook

OXFORD

 # Life long ago

Anne of Green Gables

Read Anne's account of the day her teacher tells the class he is leaving.

"I never thought you were so fond of Mr Phillips that you'd require two handkerchiefs to dry your tears just because he was going away," said Marilla.

"I don't think I was crying because I was really so very fond of him," reflected Anne. "I just cried because all the others did. It was Ruby Gillis that started it. Ruby Gillis has always declared she hated Mr Phillips, but just as soon as he got up to make his farewell speech she burst into tears. Then all the girls began to cry, one after the other. I tried to hold out, Marilla. I tried to remember the time Mr Phillips made me sit with Gil – with a boy; and the time he spelled my name without an *e* on the blackboard; and how he said I was the worst dunce he ever saw at geometry and laughed at my spelling; and all the times he had been so horrid and sarcastic; but somehow I couldn't, Marilla, and I just had to cry too."

From *Anne of Green Gables*, by L. M. Montgomery

A **Tick two of the following sentences to show which are true.**

Mr Phillips had made Anne sit with a boy in class. ☐

Mr Phillips had said that Anne was really good at geometry. ☐

Mr Phillips thought Anne couldn't spell very well. ☐

Anne thought Mr Phillips' jokes were very funny. ☐

Mr Phillips spelled Anne's name correctly on the blackboard. ☐

B Answer these questions about the extract. Give evidence from the extract.

1 How do we know Anne cried a lot when Mr Phillips said he was leaving?

_____

2 At what point did Ruby Gillis start crying?

_____

3 Why was it strange that Ruby Gillis was the first to start crying?

_____

4 Do you think Anne was really sad that Mr Phillips was leaving?

yes   no

What does she say to make you believe this?

_____

C Find the word or words in the extract which match the following meanings.

1 stop yourself from doing something

_____

2 a person who finds learning difficult

_____

3 being funny in a hard or unpleasant way

_____

4 Find two words in the extract used instead of 'said'.

_____

_____

Adverbs

A Look at the adverbs or adverbial phrases in the sentences below. Are they adverbs of place, manner or time?

1 **As soon as he got up to say his farewell speech**, she burst into tears.

This is an adverbial phrase of _____.

2 There was total silence **in the dark, cramped schoolroom**.

This is an adverbial phrase of _____.

3 "It's spelled Anne, not Ann," Anne told Mr Phillips **angrily**.

This is an adverb of _____.

B Complete these sentences, which contain adverbs or adverbial phrases, with your own ideas.

1 "_____,"cried Ruby Gillis **miserably**.

2 **The day before yesterday**, Mr Phillips told Anne that _____
_____

3 **By the warm kitchen fire**, Anne and Marilla _____
_____

C Add an adverb or adverbial phrase to complete the sentences.

1 _____, Mr Phillips made Anne sit next to Gilbert because she was talking too much.

2 The children packed up their bags and left the room _____.

3 Anne did her homework _____.

Clauses and commas

A Underline the main clause in the following sentences.

1 As Anne was so upset, she needed two handkerchiefs to dry her tears.

2 As soon as Mr Phillips stood up, she burst into tears.

3 All the girls began to cry, one after the other.

4 Four days ago, Anne spelled 'teacher' incorrectly.

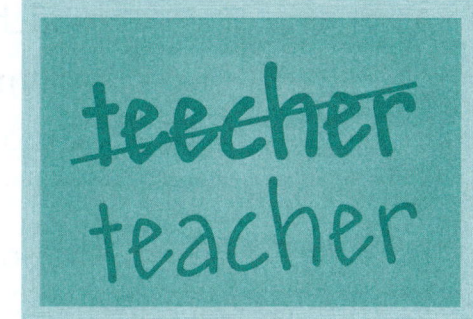

B Write three new sentences by adding different subordinate clauses to the main clause below. Use the correct punctuation.

Gilbert pulled Anne's hair (main clause)

1 _____

_____

2 _____

_____

3 _____

_____

C Finish these sentences by adding a main clause. Don't forget to add a comma in the appropriate place.

1 As it was raining _____

_____

2 As soon as the bell was rung _____

_____

3 Thinking very carefully _____

_____

4 As the teacher was obviously cross _____

_____

Irregular verbs, clauses and commas

A Add the correct verb form to the following sentences.

1 As it _____ (be) such a wet day Anne _____ (take) her umbrella when she _____ (go) to school.

2 Gilbert who _____ (be) a handsome boy _____ (go) to the same school as Anne.

3 As soon as the class _____ (have) their books on their desks the teacher _____ (be) ready to start the lesson.

4 On Sundays when there _____ (be) no school Anne and her friends _____ (go) to the river to have a picnic.

B The commas in the sentences above have all been left out. Read the sentences again, adding the commas in. You might need to add more than one comma into some of the sentences.

C Write this main clause and this subordinate clause together in one complete sentence. Don't forget to add the correct punctuation.

Mr Phillips wrote the alphabet on the blackboard (main clause)

who was the class teacher (subordinate clause)

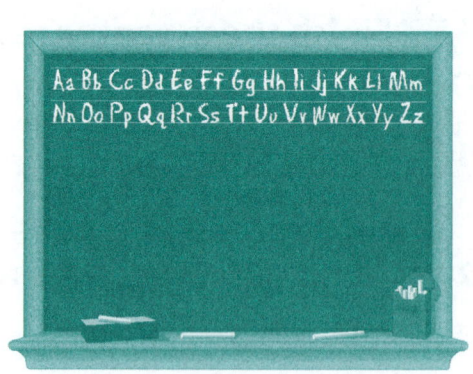

_____

_____

Self-assessment on my learning
Unit 1 Life long ago

Name _____

Date _____

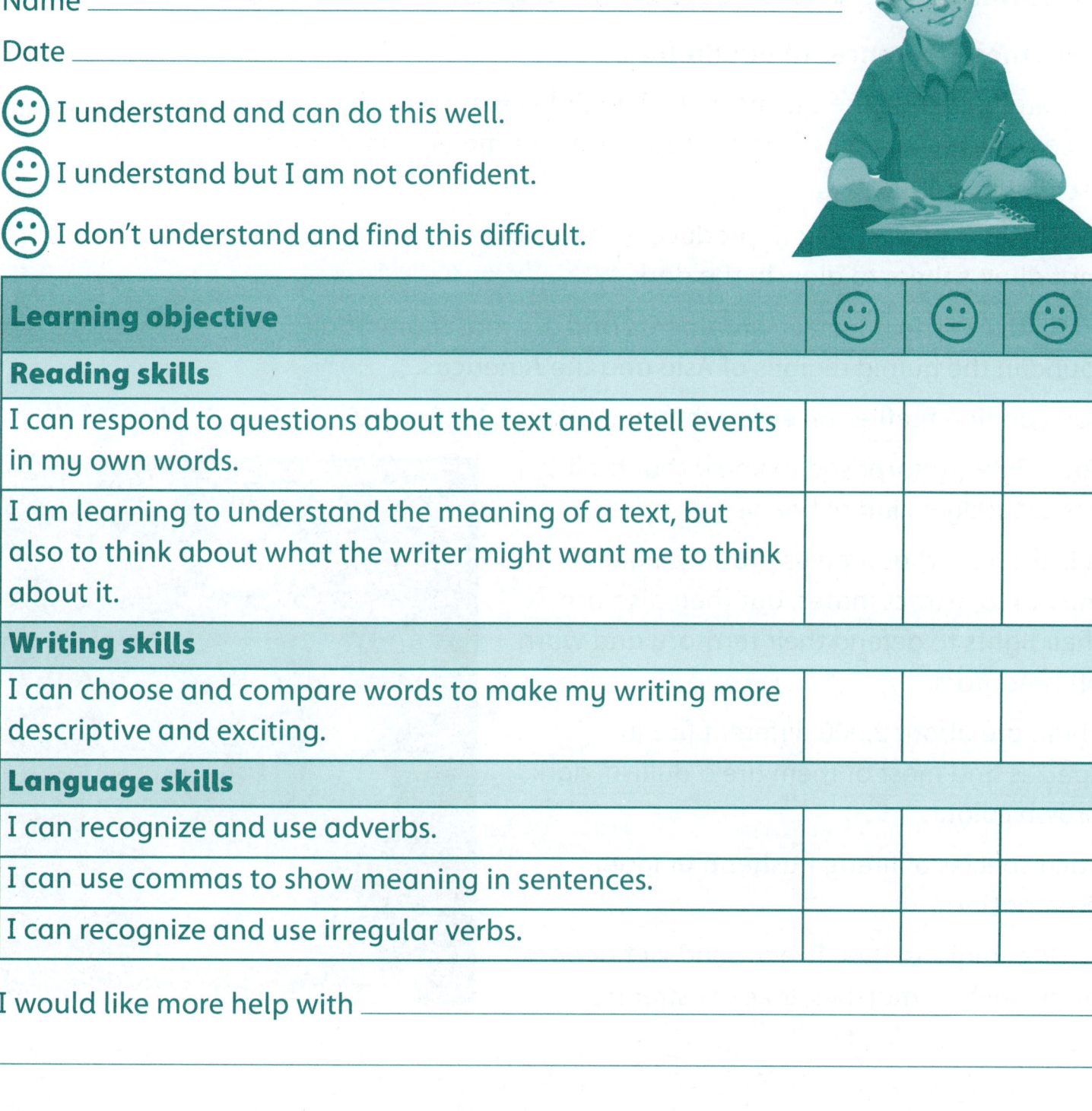

☺ I understand and can do this well.

😐 I understand but I am not confident.

☹ I don't understand and find this difficult.

Learning objective	☺	😐	☹
Reading skills			
I can respond to questions about the text and retell events in my own words.			
I am learning to understand the meaning of a text, but also to think about what the writer might want me to think about it.			
Writing skills			
I can choose and compare words to make my writing more descriptive and exciting.			
Language skills			
I can recognize and use adverbs.			
I can use commas to show meaning in sentences.			
I can recognize and use irregular verbs.			

I would like more help with _____

_____

_____

2 Beautiful bugs!

Features of non-chronological reports

Read these sentences about fireflies.

The firefly's lights are the most efficient lights in the world because 100 per cent of the energy is used for making light and no heat is produced.

Fireflies are nocturnal and produce a chemical in their bodies that allows them to glow in the dark.

They love warm, moist environments and are most commonly found in the humid regions of Asia and the Americas.

You can find fireflies on every continent except Antarctica.

You might be surprised to know that fireflies are actually a kind of beetle.

It is thought that fireflies produce light mostly to attract mates, but they also use their lights to defend their territory and warn off predators.

There are about 2,000 different firefly species and most of them are a dullish, dark brown colour.

Each species of firefly flashes a unique light pattern.

In drier regions, they live around wet or damp areas such as marshes, lakes or streams.

Writing a glossary

A Use a dictionary to create your own glossary. Match the words in bold to their meanings below.

unique   nocturnal   humid   moist   efficient

1 active at night time   _____

2 slightly wet   _____

3 having a high amount of water in the air   _____

4 performing in the best possible way   _____

5 the only one of its kind   _____

B Find three sentences from page 8 which, when grouped together, make a paragraph that answers the following questions. Make sure that you put the sentences in the correct order so that the text makes complete sense. The questions will be your subheadings.

Where do you find fireflies?

_____

_____

_____

Why do fireflies light up?

_____

_____

_____

What is a firefly?

_____

_____

_____

Adverbs

A Find the 24 adverbs hidden in this word search.

b	r	i	s	k	l	y	e	s	t	e	r	d	a	y
e	a	s	i	l	y	o	u	t	h	f	u	l	l	y
a	n	g	r	i	l	y	n	o	i	s	i	l	y	e
u	r	g	e	n	t	l	y	d	e	e	p	l	y	l
t	r	u	l	y	m	i	s	e	r	a	b	l	y	e
i	n	s	t	a	n	t	l	y	e	a	r	l	y	g
f	a	i	r	l	y	h	u	n	g	r	i	l	y	a
u	s	e	f	u	l	l	y	e	v	e	n	l	y	n
l	a	z	i	l	y	h	a	p	p	i	l	y	l	t
l	o	u	d	l	y	g	r	e	e	d	i	l	y	l
y	e	x	a	c	t	l	y	c	r	o	s	s	l	y

a_____   h_____

b_____   i_____

b_____   l_____

c_____   l_____

d_____   m_____

e_____   n_____

e_____   t_____

e_____   u_____

e_____   u_____

e_____   y_____

f_____   y_____

g_____   y_____

h_____   y_____

B Complete these sentences by using one or two of the adverbs from the word search and by adding commas in the appropriate places.

1 My aunt who was dressed very e_____ was on her way to the theatre.

2 Y_____ it was wet and windy but today the weather is t_____ wonderful.

3 "Thank you for the gift!" she said h_____.
"You have wrapped it b_____."

4 When she saw the empty sweet wrappers she i_____ knew e_____ what had happened.

5 When Joseph saw the doughnuts he h_____ grabbed one and ate it g_____.

Alphabetical order

C Put the following groups of adverbs in alphabetical order.

1 hopelessly, greedily, happily, joyfully, hungrily

_____ _____ _____ _____ _____

2 warmly, zealously, quietly, oddly, vastly

_____ _____ _____ _____ _____

3 cheerfully, coldly, curiously, casually, cleverly

_____ _____ _____ _____ _____

4 softly, slowly, strictly, shyly, smoothly

_____ _____ _____ _____ _____

5 rarely, regularly, rudely, really, roughly

_____ _____ _____ _____ _____

Writing a non-chronological report

A Look at the paragraphs you wrote about the firefly on page 9. Answer these questions about the common features of non-chronological reports.

1 What would be a good **title** for your report? _____

2 What type of sentences are the **subheadings**? _____

3 Is **formal language** used? Give an example. _____

_____

4 Are **adverbs or adverbial phrases** used? Give an example. _____

5 Are **connectives** used to join ideas? Give an example. _____

B Now answer these questions about your report.

1 What is a glossary? _____

2 What tense is the report written in? _____

3 Which personal pronoun is used to make the report more informal and reader-friendly? _____

C Without looking at the report again, write a paragraph of three to four sentences about the firefly in your own words.

Self-assessment on my learning

Unit 2 Beautiful bugs!

Name _____

Date _____

😊 I understand and can do this well.

😐 I understand but I am not confident.

☹ I don't understand and find this difficult.

Learning objective	😊	😐	☹
Reading skills			
I can note key words and phrases to identify the main points in a non-fiction text.			
I can recognize different types of non-fiction text and their main features.			
Writing skills			
I understand how paragraphs are used to organise ideas.			
I have practised writing a non-chronological report.			
Language skills			
I can recognize and use adverbs.			
I can put words into alphabetical order.			

I would like more help with _____

_____

_____

_____

3 Tricks and truth

A play script of *Aladdin*

Read this scene based on the traditional story of Aladdin.

Characters

Aladdin, a carefree, lazy boy, who never does anything to help his poor, widowed mother.

Stranger, a mysterious old man.

SCENE 1

(In the street, where a young boy is playing with his friends.)

Stranger	*(approaching the boy)* Excuse me, young man. Are you the son of Mustapha, the tailor?
Aladdin	Yes… but he died ages ago.
Stranger	*(grabbing Aladdin's hand)* Oh dear, dear, boy! I am your uncle. I could tell straight away that you were my dear brother's son – you look so like him.
Aladdin	Really?
Stranger	*(happily)* Of course! Now, run along home and tell your mother I'm on my way to visit her.

A Answer these questions, using information from the play script.

1 Which adjectives are used to describe Aladdin's character?

_____ and _____

2 Was Aladdin a good son?

yes   no

What evidence from the text do you have for your answer?

_____

3 What was Aladdin doing when the stranger approached him?

_____

4 Why was Aladdin surprised to be asked about his father?

_____

5 What did the stranger do when he found out who Aladdin was?

_____

6 How does the stranger say he knew who Aladdin was?

_____

7 Is 'happily' an adjective or an adverb? _____

B Using the play script on page 14 to help you, write down five features of play scripts.

1 _____

2 _____

3 _____

4 _____

5 _____

Powerful verbs and adverbs

A Use one of the powerful verbs below to fill each of the gaps. Use the play script on page 14 to help you.

1 A mysterious old man _____ over to Aladdin.

2 "Are you the son of Mustapha, the tailor?" _____ the stranger.

3 The question _____ Aladdin, because his father had died years before.

4 "Oh dear, dear, boy!" _____ the old man. "I am your uncle!"

5 "Now _____ off home and _____ your mother I'm on my way to visit her."

inform   gushed   questioned   shuffled   dash   bewildered

B Complete the play script below by including a powerful adverb in the brackets.

Stranger   (_____) Excuse me, young man. Are you the son of Mustapha, the tailor?

Aladdin   (_____) Yes… but he died ages ago.

Stranger   (_____) Oh dear, dear, boy! I am your uncle. I could tell straight away that you were my dear brother's son – you look so like him.

Aladdin   (_____) Really?

Stranger   (_____) Of course! Now, run along home and tell your mother I'm on my way to visit her.

suspiciously   uncertainly   joyously   cheerfully   politely

Irregular verbs

A Put these irregular verbs into the correct form of the past tense.

Aladdin _____ (run) home and _____ (tell) his mother that he _____ (bring) interesting news.

Aladdin _____ (say) that his uncle _____ (see) him in the street and immediately _____ (become) excited because he recognized who Aladdin _____. (be)

Aladdin _____ (say) he _____ (come) home straight away to tell her.

His mother _____ (speak) suspiciously and asked Aladdin if he _____ (think) the man really _____ (be) his uncle.

Aladdin replied that he _____ (know) that the man really _____ (be) his uncle and she would too when she _____ (meet) him.

So Aladdin's mother _____ (make) some delicious food which _____ (smell) beautiful.

When the uncle _____ (come), they all _____ (sit) down and _____ (eat) a wonderful meal.

B Make sentences in the past tense using the following irregular verbs.
hear   write   ride   wake   buy   grow

_____

_____

_____

_____

_____

_____

_____

_____

Writing a play script

A Complete the play script below using your own ideas. Try to build up the excitement in the scene. Compare the scene on page 14 and the text on page 17 to help you.

SCENE 2
(In Aladdin's home.)

Aladdin   *(rushing in, excitedly)* Mother! Great news! I just met my uncle in the street!

Aladdin' mother *(suspiciously)* _____

_____

Aladdin   (_____) _____

_____

Aladdin's mother (_____) _____

_____

_____ (_____) _____

_____

_____ (_____) _____

_____

_____ (_____) _____

_____

Self-assessment on my learning
Unit 3 Tricks and truth

Name _____

Date _____

🙂 I understand and can do this well.

😐 I understand but I am not confident.

🙁 I don't understand and find this difficult.

Learning objective	🙂	😐	🙁
Reading skills			
I have practised reading play scripts, exploring how scenes are built up.			
I can respond to questions about the text and retell events in my own words.			
Writing skills			
I am able to choose and compare words, such as powerful verbs, to make writing more descriptive and/or exciting.			
I can use alternatives for overused words like *said*.			
Language skills			
I can recognize and use adverbs.			
I can recognize and use irregular verbs in the past tense.			

I would like more help with _____

_____

_____

_____

4 Fantastic journeys

Apostrophes

A Write the following contractions in full.

aren't _____	can't _____	didn't _____
won't _____	you'd _____	he'll _____
it's _____	isn't _____	I've _____
I'd _____	there's _____	we're _____
don't _____	that's _____	who'd _____
you've _____	they're _____	she'd _____

B Put possessive apostrophes in these sentences. (Remember: In a plural noun, the possessive apostrophe comes after the *s*.)

1 The dogs basket was very smelly.

2 The dogs baskets were very smelly.

3 The girls coats are hung up in the cloakroom.

4 Roberts school bag was very heavy.

5 The childrens workbooks were kept in class.

Explain why 'children' is different to the other nouns. _____

_____

C In the sentences below, say whether each apostrophe is used for a contraction or to show possession.

1 I **can't** find **Nina's** shoes.

2 **Who's** going to **Ali's** house after school?

3 **That's** my **friend's** picture.

4 **What's** the new **girl's** name?

A fantasy story

A Read the following story extract. You will notice that there are no apostrophes. Add in the apostrophes that have been missed out.

Mitras picture was almost finished but just needed a <u>pinch</u> of silver glitter to make it perfect. She looked at Alisas picture and could see whod used up all the glitter. Shed have to have a look in the classrooms store cupboard. Thered bound to be some, somewhere, if she <u>rummaged</u> hard enough. When she entered the small room, she was surprised to see a door slightly <u>ajar</u> at the back of it.

"Im sure that wasnt there before," she thought. Curious, she <u>shuffled</u> over and pushed the door open.

"How strange! Theres a tree." Mitra walked through the door and found herself in the middle of a pine forest, coated in thick, soft, white snow and <u>bathed</u> in silvery moonlight.

Mitra was <u>intrigued</u>. One minute she was in the classroom in daylight, the next in the middle of a wintry forest at night time.

"I wish Id brought my coat!" she thought.

B Match the underlined words in the text with a word or words with a similar meaning from below.

open   looked   moved slowly   interested   covered   a tiny bit

C This extract is from a fantasy story. How do you know this is fantasy fiction?

_____

_____

Similes

A Choose the best adjective below, to complete the similes.

flat   dry   pure   sweet   sharp   quick   light   black

as _____ as lightning   as _____ as snow

as _____ as honey   as _____ as a bone

as _____ as a pancake   as _____ as a feather

as _____ as a razor   as _____ as coal

B Complete these similes with your own ideas.

as busy as a _____   as free as a _____

as hungry as a _____   as slow as a _____

as strong as a _____   as quiet as a _____

C Match the simile on the left with its definition on the right.

as snug as a bug in a rug   very, very old indeed

as old as the hills   very safe and secure

as nutty as a fruitcake   very comfortable and cosy

as safe as houses   completely crazy

More fantasy fiction

Read this extract, which continues the fantasy story from page 21.

Mitra edged further into the forest and further away from the store cupboard door.

A quarter of an hour later, she was as cold as ice, so she turned around to return to the classroom. Suddenly, as quick as a flash, a squirrel, dressed as grandly as a king, jumped out in front of her.

"Halt, spy of the snow queen!" he squeaked.

"Oh my, I've never seen a talking squirrel before, how sweet!" smiled Mitra.

"Sweet?" screeched the squirrel, as angry as a little raging bull, "I'll show you who's sweet!"

"Captain Omerlon, Captain, stop!" came a youthful voice from the trees behind. "This is the human girl that the wise man foresaw would be sent to us. She will save us from the snow queen and free our people."

Then, through the trees, appeared a handsome young prince, with hair as golden as the sun. He was sitting on a unicorn, as pure as snow, and surrounded by a small army of badgers, foxes and squirrels running beside him, on their two back legs.

A Underline the six similes used in the story. Choose four of them and use them in your own sentences below.

1 _____

2 _____

3 _____

4 _____

B Find a word or words in the extract with a similar meaning to the words below.

good-looking _____

go back to _____

predicted _____

moved _____

stop _____

yelled _____

C Write down five features of fantasy writing and find an example of each of the features you choose in the story about Mitra.

Example: There are often fantastical beasts – the prince is sitting on a unicorn.

1 _____

2 _____

3 _____

4 _____

5 _____

Self-assessment on my learning
Unit 4 Fantastic journeys

Name _____

Date _____

😊 I understand and can do this well.

😐 I understand but I am not confident.

☹️ I don't understand and find this difficult.

Learning objective	😊	😐	☹️
Reading skills			
I understand how settings and characters are built up from details and can identify key words and phrases.			
I can apply what I already know to help me read unfamiliar words.			
Writing skills			
I can recognize and use similes.			
Language skills			
I can recognize and use apostrophes to show possession and contractions.			

I would like more help with _____

_____

_____

5 Amazing animals

A newspaper report

A Complete the following newspaper report by adding a word or words from the list below. Use a dictionary to help you.

> membership   overseas   purpose
> generation   sit back   aware
> extinct   survival

School Children Earn Their Stripes

<u>Fellow students</u> in Ludhiana, India, have decided that they are not happy to

_____ and watch the tiger become _____ in their lifetimes

so they have come up with their own <u>initiative</u> to save this magnificent

beast. They have created the 'earn your stripes' society with the <u>sole</u>

_____ of bringing young minds together to develop different ways

to save the Punjab tigers.

"Tigers are on the <u>verge</u> of extinction," says Nandan Kapur, society member.
"There is a need for people to be _____ of the importance of tigers
and what their _____ means to us. We
want the next _____ to have the same
honour we have of being able to see tigers in
their natural <u>habitat</u>."

So far, the society boasts 1,723 members and
its _____ is growing every day. If you
are interested in earning your own stripes, you
do not have to live in Ludhiana to become a
member. You can become an _____
member and you will receive regular <u>updates</u>
about the society's policies.

B Which of the underlined words in the newspaper report has a similar meaning to the words below?

peers _____   point _____

territory _____   new idea _____

news _____   single _____

C Answer these questions about the newspaper report.

1 Who created the society?

_____

2 'Earn your stripes' is an idiom that means 'to prove yourself'. Can you think of another reason the title of the report is *School Children Earn Their Stripes*?

_____

3 Do you think that this article was written for a student magazine or an adult newspaper? Explain your answer.

_____

_____

Apostrophes and adjectives

A Add the missing apostrophes to the following sentences.

1 Tigers natural habitat is being destroyed.

2 A tigers footprint was found next to the well.

3 The childrens lesson was about the importance of saving the tiger.

4 The tiger cubs eyes open when they are about ten days old.

B Put the adjectives in the brackets into either the comparative or the superlative form.

1 Cheetahs are _____ (fast) than tigers, but tigers are _____ (big) than cheetahs.

2 The tiger is a _____ (endangered) animal than the cheetah.

3 The _____ (dangerous) problem the tiger faces is the loss of its natural habitat.

4 The _____ (hungry) a tiger, the more dangerous it is.

C Choose an appropriate strong adjective to complete these sentences.

1 After playing football in the rain, Michal's kit wasn't just dirty, it was _____. (horrible, filthy, unclean, awful, creased)

2 When Sophie fell in the stream, her clothes weren't just wet, they were _____. (damp, soggy, moist, soaking, bad)

3 The baby squirrel wasn't just small, it was _____. (little, minute, short, slight)

4 When Andre broke a window, his dad wasn't just angry, he was _____. (furious, cross, peeved, upset, annoyed)

Metaphors and similes

A Say whether the following sentences contain a metaphor or a simile.

1   A blanket of snow covered the valley.

2   The clouds were as white as snow.

3   Abraham runs like the wind.

4   My little brother is a monkey!

5   Aini was the light of her mother's life.

B In your own words, explain what each of the sentences above mean.

1   _____

2   _____

3   _____

4   _____

5   _____

C Complete these metaphors by using one of the words below.

cold   crop   heart   sly   rock

1   My grandfather is so kind, I think he has a _____ of gold.

2   Joshi was going to sing a solo in front of all the parents, but then he got _____ feet and couldn't do it.

3   Guilia often plays tricks on her brothers. She's such a _____ fox.

4   Each year, a new _____ of students enters the college.

5   I can always depend on Riko to support me. He is my _____.

Writing a newspaper report

A Write down five features of a newspaper report.

1 _____

2 _____

3 _____

4 _____

5 _____

B Using the information below, write a report about tigers. Include a made-up quote from Rajesh Kumar, the Tiger Conservation Society leader.

In an effort to increase India's tiger population, the Tiger Conservation Society has asked the government to create seven more tiger reserves. This would take the total number of reserves in the country to 49.

The number of tigers in India has gone up from 1,411 in 2006 to 1,706 in 2010.

The government will give financial help to people who are willing to move out of protected areas.

India has more than half of the world's population of tigers still living in the wild.

_____

_____

_____

_____

_____

_____

_____

Self-assessment on my learning

Unit 5 Amazing animals

Name _____

Date _____

😊 I understand and can do this well.

😐 I understand but I am not confident.

☹ I don't understand and find this difficult.

Learning objective	😊	😐	☹
Reading skills			
I can recognize different types of non-fiction text and their main features.			
I can understand the main ideas of an account and respond to them.			
I understand how newspaper reports engage the reader.			
Writing skills			
I understand how the layout and presentation of writing helps to get across ideas.			
I have practised writing a newspaper report.			
Language skills			
I can use the apostrophe to show possession.			
I understand how different adjectives can strengthen meaning.			

I would like more help with _____

_____

_____

_____

6 Families of the world

A poem about family

Read this poem.

My sister lives in Singapore,
Cousin Kate's in Cork,
My auntie lives in Ecuador,
Her nephew's in New York.
Madeline's in Manchester,
Michael's in Milan,
Winnie works in Winchester,
Joan lives in Japan.
The twins have moved to Tuscany,
Ronald lives in Rome,
Granny's gone to Germany –
And me? I live at home!

Catherine and Laurence Anholt

 This poem doesn't have a title. What title would you give the poem?

_____

B Find the words in the poem which rhyme with the places below.

Singapore _____   Rome _____

York _____   Milan _____

Manchester _____   Tuscany _____

C

1 Match up the rhyming pairs of countries below.

Gambia   Bermuda

Barbuda   Uganda

Rwanda   Spain

Albania   Zambia

Ukraine   Romania

2 Now make up some rhyming pairs of places yourself. They could be countries, cities, towns or villages.

_____

_____

_____

_____

_____

_____

Alliteration

A Underline all the examples of alliteration in the poem on page 32. Remember, alliteration is when the same letter or sound is repeated at the beginning of several words. *Example:* sing a song of sixpence or whisper words of wisdom.

B Complete these sentences with a name that adds to the alliteration.

Example: <u>Marlon</u> moved to Mongolia.

_____ flew to Finland.

_____ immigrated to India.

_____ joined Joe in Jordan.

_____ happily hiked to Haiti.

_____ took a train to Thailand.

_____ bused beyond Bulgaria.

_____ sailed to sunny Spain.

C Use the names of your family or friends to make seven sentences of your own. Make sure they show amazing alliteration!

1 _____

2 _____

3 _____

4 _____

5 _____

6 _____

7 _____

Writing a poem

A Read the poem on page 32 out loud. Make sure that you briefly pause at the commas, and briefly stop at the full stops. Notice the rhythm of the poem. After how many lines does the full stop come each time? _____

B Using the exercises you completed in this chapter, fill in the gaps below to make up your own poem about your friends and family. They can be silly sentences, but try to include rhyme and alliteration.

Example:
Katarina lives in Kathmandu,
my sister lives in a shoe.

_____ lives in _____,

_____ _____ in _____,

_____ lives in _____,

_____ _____ in _____.

_____ in _____,

_____ in _____,

_____ lives in _____ –

And me? I live _____.

Different language techniques

A Which of these techniques is used in the sentences below?

| alliteration | metaphor | rhyme | simile |

Example: The cat in the hat sat on the mat. <u>rhyme</u>

1 Ali ate an apple on an August afternoon. _____

2 Wrens in the fens live in dens. _____

3 He was as thin as a beanstalk. _____

4 There's a lizard in a blizzard. _____

5 Julia's head was spinning with ideas. _____

6 Atif was so tired, he slept like a log. _____

7 Ben barbecued Belinda's banana. _____

8 My brother is a bear with a sore head when he first wakes up. _____

B Think of a word to complete these similes and metaphors.

1 My best friend is as _____ as a rock.

2 Kim is as sweet as _____.

3 Carolina has the voice of a _____.

4 I'm as hungry as a _____.

C Write one simile and one metaphor about yourself.

Simile: _____

Metaphor: _____

Self-assessment on my learning
Unit 6 Families of the world

Name _____

Date _____

☺ I understand and can do this well.

☺ I understand but I am not confident.

☹ I don't understand and find this difficult.

Learning objective	☺	☺	☹
Reading skills			
I recognize all the punctuation marks and respond to them when reading.			
I have practised reading silently and reading aloud.			
Writing skills			
I can express a personal response to a text and link characters and settings to personal experience.			
Language skills			
I recognize and can use imagery and figurative language in poetry, including alliteration and simile.			

I would like more help with _____

_____

_____

_____

7 All together!

Reading comprehension

Read this extract.

My Best Friend

I first met my best friend at school seven years ago. My teacher had told me that there was to be a new girl called Belen and that I should look after her. She told me to go to the head teacher's office to collect Belen and bring her back to the classroom.

Walking through the school, I felt very excited. I started to think about the qualities I wanted my new friend to have. She would be <u>bold</u>, lively, and lots of fun. We were going to have such adventures together!

When I finally arrived at the office, the <u>sullen</u>, awkward girl waiting for me was nothing like I had imagined. She took one <u>timid</u> glance at me, and then quickly looked down at her feet again. She was small and skinny with a pale, freckly face that was made all the paler and thinner by her thick, straight, pale brown hair.

"Hello, Belen," I said <u>coldly</u>, barely able to contain my disappointment.

"My name is Maria, not Belen. Belen is my second name," she replied resentfully.

"Huh, great start," I thought to myself as, without another word, I turned and started walking back to the classroom, with Maria following reluctantly behind.

Seven years later, I can say that Maria is my best friend! We have had so many great times together. It just goes to show that first impressions can be wrong!

A **Answer these questions about the extract.**

1 Why is the narrator excited as she walks through the school to the head teacher's office?

_____

2 What qualities does the narrator hope Maria will have?

_____

3 Why is the narrator disappointed when she meets Maria?

_____

4 Is the narrator wrong to be disappointed? How do you know?

_____

5 What mistake did the teacher make about the new girl?

_____

B **Match an underlined word in the text with the meaning below. Use a dictionary to help you.**

1 in an unfriendly way, heartlessly _____

2 fearless, not hesitating _____

3 miserable, gloomy _____

4 shy, no self-confidence _____

C **Describe what Maria looks like.**

_____

_____

_____

_____

Homophones

A Match a word from the left with its homophone on the right.

new	won
saw	they're
through	too
their	fare
fair	weight
two	knew
wait	threw
one	sore

B Fill the gaps with words from above to complete these sentences.

1 Amy _____ the ball up in the air, and it went _____ the basketball ring.

2 I have _____ brothers and my best friend has _____ brothers _____.

3 The children are packing because _____ going to stay for a week at _____ granny's house.

C Write a homophone for the following words.

ate _____   so _____   aloud _____

be _____   bean _____   pain _____

Sentence types

A Look at the sentences below. For each one, write whether it is a question, an exclamation, a statement or a command.

Example: Stop talking now! <u>command</u>

1 Help! _____

2 It's nine o'clock. Go to bed!
_____ and _____

3 What are you doing? I need your help. _____ and _____

4 Is that your painting? It's brilliant! _____ and _____

B Write the following sentences as a command, question, exclamation or statement. Add the correct punctuation.

Example: Tell the boy to sit down now. <u>Sit down, now!</u>

1 Ask Miyo what Kaito looks like.

_____

2 Tell the teacher how old you are.

_____

3 Tell the girl to stop making so much noise.

_____

4 You have dropped a heavy book on your toe. What do you say?

_____

C Read the extract *My Best Friend* again. Write questions to ask Maria using the following words. Remember to use the correct punctuation.

What _____

Where _____

When _____

Writing good character descriptions

A Answer these questions.

1 List four things a good character description might include.

_____

_____

_____

_____

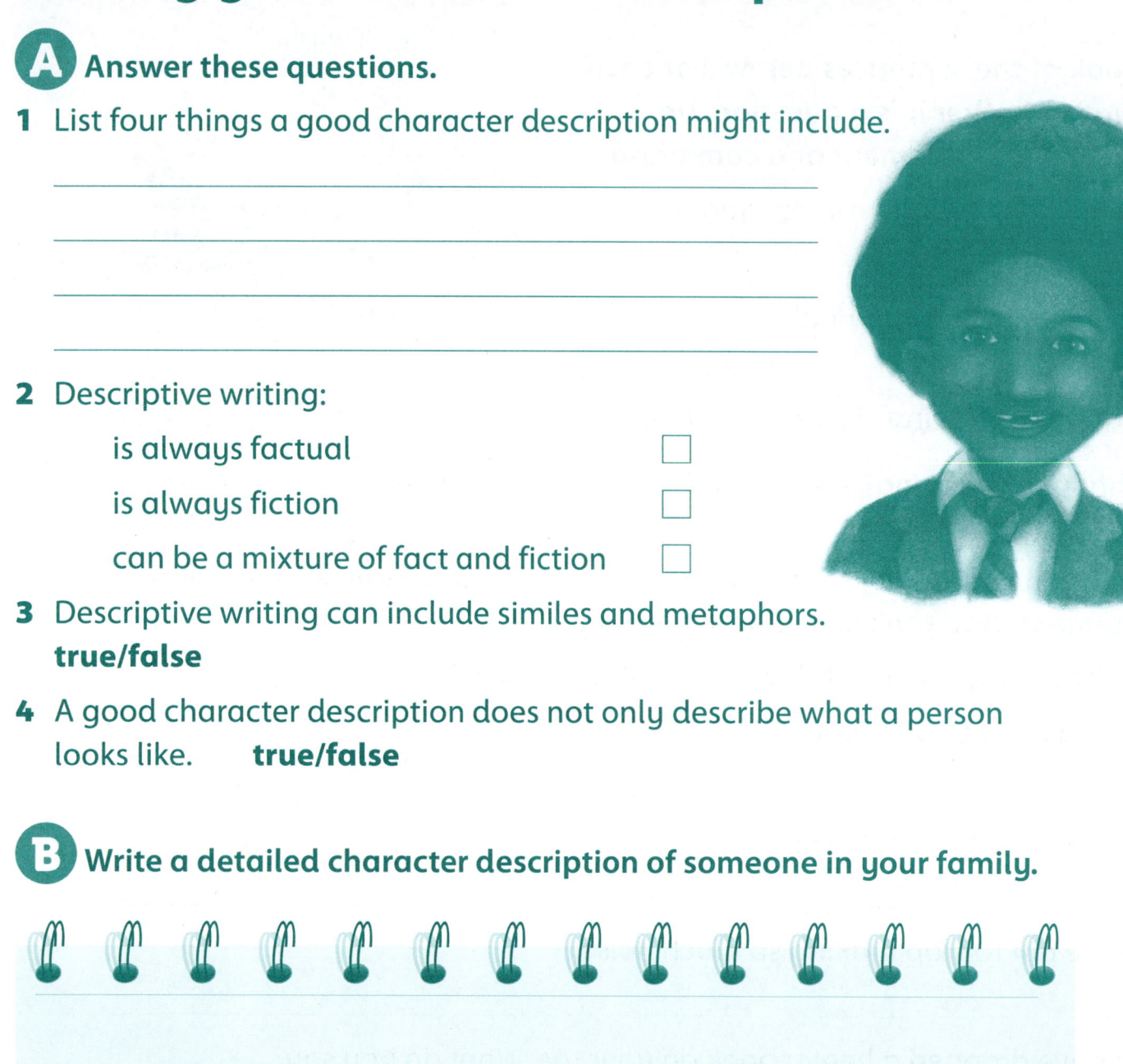

2 Descriptive writing:

is always factual ☐

is always fiction ☐

can be a mixture of fact and fiction ☐

3 Descriptive writing can include similes and metaphors.
true/false

4 A good character description does not only describe what a person looks like. **true/false**

B Write a detailed character description of someone in your family.

_____

_____

_____

_____

_____

Self-assessment on my learning
Unit 7 All together!

Name _____

Date _____

😊 I understand and can do this well.

😐 I understand but I am not confident.

☹️ I don't understand and find this difficult.

Learning objective	😊	😐	☹️
Reading skills			
I can respond to questions about the text and retell events in my own words.			
I understand how characters are built up from details and am able to pick out the important words and phrases.			
Writing skills			
I am learning to understand the meaning of a text, but also to think about what the writer might want me to think about it.			
I can write a description of a person using detail to capture the reader's imagination.			
Language skills			
I can recognize homophones.			
I understand the grammar of different types of sentences.			
I recognize and can use a range of end-of-sentence punctuation correctly.			

I would like more help with _____

_____

_____

8 World of water

Writing an explanatory text

Read the five paragraphs below about the dragonfly.

The dragonfly eggs hatch into <u>nymphs</u>. Dragonfly nymphs live in the water while they grow and develop into dragonflies. This can take up to four years to complete. Dragonfly nymphs live in ponds because the water is calmer than in streams or rivers.

The young dragonfly will look for a mate and the whole cycle begins again. Adult dragonflies live for about two months.

In springtime, once the nymph is fully grown, it will crawl out of the water up the <u>stem</u> of a plant. The nymph will shed its skin on to the stem of the plant and will then be a young dragonfly.

A male and a female dragonfly will mate while they are flying in the air. Afterwards, the female dragonfly will lay her eggs on a plant leaf in the water. The life cycle has begun.

A dragonfly has a <u>lifespan</u> of more than one year, but very little of it is actually as an adult dragonfly. There are three stages in a dragonfly's life cycle: the egg, the nymph and the adult dragonfly.

A Make a glossary by matching the underlined words in the text to the meanings below.

1 the length of a whole lifetime _____

2 the part of a plant that supports the leaves _____

3 young dragonflies _____

B Rearrange the paragraphs about the dragonfly into the correct order to create an explanatory text about the life cycle of a dragonfly. Add in the subheadings below.

The nymph stage   **The life cycle of a dragonfly**

The egg stage   **The adult dragonfly**

Connectives

A Look back at the extract about the life cycle of a dragonfly.

1 Find four examples of connectives.

_____   _____   _____   _____

2 Find one example of a time connective.   _____

B Write all the time connectives from the box below in the clock shape.

| therefore   firstly   next |
| because   then   later |
| as a result   after   since |
| in addition   now   when   once |
| however   although   while |
| finally   unbelievably   until |

C Add a connective from exercise B into each of the gaps below. (There might be more than one possibility.)

_____ the dragonflies mate. _____, the female lays the eggs on a leaf in a pond. _____ the eggs hatch, they become nymphs. The nymphs live in the pond _____ they develop into dragonflies. _____ the nymphs shed their skin to become dragonflies.

Prefixes, suffixes and roots

A Make as many words as you can by adding suffixes or prefixes to the following root words.

1 taste _____

2 help _____

3 comfort _____

4 like _____

5 move _____

6 respect _____

B Complete the sentences by filling the gaps with a word that comes from the root word in brackets.

1 I got rid of the old chairs because they were _____. (comfort)

2 My mother told my brother that he was being rude and _____. (respect)

3 I was surprised to hear they are twins because they are very _____ (like) each other.

4 Before she went to sleep, she _____ (move) her slippers.

C Use a dictionary to make three words from each of the following roots. The meaning of the root is in brackets.

bio (life)

audi (hear)

tele (at a distance)

_____   _____   _____

_____   _____   _____

_____   _____   _____

Writing a persuasive text

A **Read the beginning of this letter.**

1 What is the purpose of the letter?

_____

_____

2 What type of letter is it?

_____

3 Use the connectives and the facts below to add another paragraph to the letter.

> Dear Mr Cable,
>
> I am writing to you on behalf of my village primary school. We have been told that a building company has proposed to build 20 new houses on the marshland on the outskirts of our village. We strongly recommend that you reject these proposals ...

Apart from that	**First of all**
What is more	**Anyway**

- Great natural beauty and home to a variety of wildlife.

- Home to a dragonfly that is nearly extinct in this country.

- Every year, Year 3 students do a biology project based on the marshland.

- Not enough facilities in the village or space in the school for 20 new families.

_____

_____

_____

_____

_____

_____

B **Add a concluding paragraph summing up all you have written and restating your own opinion.**

_____

_____

_____

Self-assessment on my learning

Unit 8 World of water

Name _____

Date _____

☺ I understand and can do this well.

😐 I understand but I am not confident.

☹ I don't understand and find this difficult.

Learning objective	☺	😐	☹
Reading skills			
I can recognize different types of non-fiction text and their main features.			
I understand how persuasive writing is used to convince a reader.			
I understand how paragraphs are used to organize ideas.			
Writing skills			
I can present a point of view in ordered points.			
I can show awareness of the reader by writing in an appropriate style.			
Language skills			
I understand the use of connectives to structure an argument.			
I recognize and can use prefixes and suffixes.			
I recognize and can use words with common roots.			

I would like more help with _____

_____

_____

_____

9 Poems for all seasons

A poem about changing seasons

THE TREE AND THE POOL

"I don't want my leaves to drop," said the tree.
"I don't want to freeze," said the pool.
"I don't want to smile," said the sombre man,
"Or ever to cry," said the Fool.

"I don't want to open," said the bud,
"I don't want to end," said the night.
"I don't want to rise," said the neap-tide, *
"Or ever to fall," said the kite.

They wished and they murmured and whispered,
They said that to change was a crime,
Then a voice from nowhere answered.
"You must do what I say," said Time.

Brian Patten

* A neap-tide comes twice a month, in the first and third quarters of the moon.

A **Find a word in the poem that matches the following meanings.**

1 spoke quietly or unclearly _____

2 serious or gloomy _____

3 the part of a plant that develops into a leaf or a flower _____

4 a clown or someone who tells jokes _____

B **The poet has used different imagery to make the reader think about the weather and changing seasons. Find examples of the following.**

autumn _____

winter _____

spring _____

a windy day _____

C **Write down three things that are the same in the first verse and the second verse.**

1 _____

2 _____

3 _____

Spellings and sounds
Odd one out

A For each list below, underline the part of the word that has the same letters. Then circle the word in which these letters are pronounced differently.

Example:

f<u>owl</u> (bowl) t<u>owel</u> <u>owl</u>

1 loud shout pour round

2 dear beard fear learn

3 although cough though dough

4 love move above gloves

5 eight weight height neighbour

6 oar oat coach soak

7 jewel blew sew knew

8 dice notice slice iceberg

9 shall all hallway wall

10 caught naughty daughter laughter

B Underline the word which rhymes with the examples given.

fair   tear (water coming from your eye)

           tear (to rip something)

so   bow (to bend your knee or body)

           bow (a decorative ribbon)

froze   close (shut the door)

           close (not far away)

seed   lead (a heavy metal)

           lead (to show someone the way)

C **Write the two different meanings of the words below, which are spelled the same but pronounced differently.**

row _____

_____

wind _____

_____

excuse _____

_____

object _____

_____

minute _____

_____

refuse _____

_____

present _____

_____

Writing a poem

A Look again at the poem on page 50. Write some similar sentences using the clues in brackets below.

Example: (summer) "I don't want <u>to dry up</u>," said the puddle.

1 (autumn) "We don't want _____," said the flowers.

2 (winter) "I don't want _____," said the river.

3 (morning) "We don't want _____," said the stars.

4 (dusk) "I don't want _____," said the Sun.

5 (spring) "I don't want _____," said the snowman.

B Now write a poem of your own. Use the correct punctuation and try to find two nouns that rhyme for lines 2 and 4.

Example: "I don't want to wake up," said the bear.
　　　　"I don't want to go to sleep," said the hare.

"I don't want _____ said the _____

I don't want _____ said the _____

I don't want _____ said the _____

Or _____ said the _____

Self-assessment on my learning

Unit 9 Poems for all seasons

Name _____

Date _____

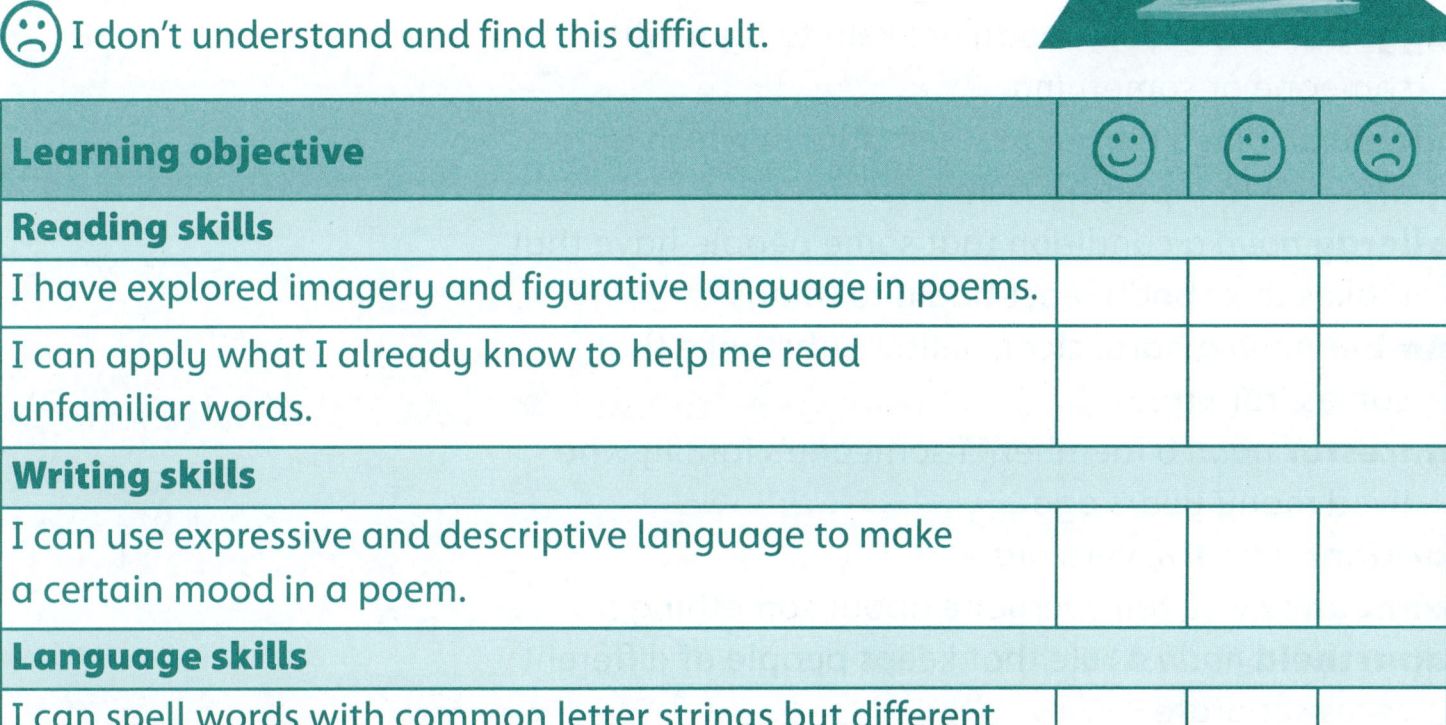

😊 I understand and can do this well.

😐 I understand but I am not confident.

☹ I don't understand and find this difficult.

Learning objective	😊	😐	☹
Reading skills			
I have explored imagery and figurative language in poems.			
I can apply what I already know to help me read unfamiliar words.			
Writing skills			
I can use expressive and descriptive language to make a certain mood in a poem.			
Language skills			
I can spell words with common letter strings but different pronunciations.			

I would like more help with _____

_____

_____

_____

Word Cloud dictionary

Aa

abolish *verb* get rid of something so that it does not happen or exist anymore

accomplish *verb* do something successfully

accuse *verb* say that someone has done something wrong

admire *verb* look at something and like it

aggressive *adjective* ready or likely to fight with someone or something

algebra *noun* a part of mathematics in which letters are used to represent numbers

allergy *noun* a condition that some people have that makes their body react badly to things

amber *noun* a hard, clear, yellow substance that comes from trees

ancestor *noun* a member of someone's family who lived many years ago

ancient *adjective* very old

announce *verb* tell everyone about something

apartheid *noun* a rule that keeps people of different races separate

Arctic *noun* the area around the North Pole

Bb

billowing *adjective* moving or flowing like waves in the sea

bleakening *adjective* bare, cold and dreary

brute *noun* a cruel person

Cc

captive *adjective* imprisoned or kept in one place

caress *verb* touch someone or something gently and fondly

century *noun* a unit of time of one hundred years

cleave *verb* split or cause to split

coin *noun* a metal piece of money

column *noun* a piece of writing that appears regularly in a newspaper or magazine

culture *noun* the language, customs, food, art and music of a group of people

customer *noun* someone who buys something in a shop

Dd

dachshund *noun* a long-bodied, short-legged breed of dog

dale *noun* a valley

damage *noun* harm or breakage

decade *noun* a period of ten years

demand *noun* the desire or need for something

dictation *noun* saying words out loud while someone else writes them down

disgraceful *adjective* very bad or unacceptable

distinctive *adjective* clearly different from others and easy to recognise

distinguished *adjective* successful and much admired by other people

drawstring *noun* a string or ribbon running through an item of clothing or a bag, which can be pulled to close or tighten it

dreamland *noun* an imagined or unreal world

drench *verb* soak someone or something with water

Ee

enchanted *adjective* magical and charming

evaporate *verb* change from liquid into steam or vapour (gas)

exaggerate *verb* make something seem greater than it is

expedition *noun* a journey with a destination, usually made in order to do something
expensive *adjective* costing a lot of money
explorer *noun* a person who goes on adventures and makes discoveries

Ff
filter *verb* pass something through something else to remove unwanted substances
friendship *noun* being friends with someone

Gg
generous-looking *adjective* looking large or ready to give or share

Hh
headline *noun* the title of a newspaper article
hollow *noun* a hole in something
hooked *adjective* having hooks (pieces of curved metal for catching on to things)

Ii
illusion *noun* something that looks real, but isn't
imagination *noun* the ability to form pictures and ideas in your mind
imagine *verb* picture something in your mind
instinct *noun* a typical pattern of behaviour in animals
Inupiat *noun* the language of a group of Inuit people living in northern Alaska

Jj
jingle *verb* make a light, ringing sound

Ll
law *noun* a rule that people in a society have to follow
leafy *adjective* covered with or having leaves
lineage *noun* direct descent from an ancestor

Mm

mammal *noun* a warm-blooded animal that has hair or fur; the female usually gives birth to live young and feeds them with her own milk

migration *noun* the movement of people or animals from one area or country to another

mingle *verb* mix together

Oo

oasis *noun* a place in a desert where there is water, and where trees and plants grow

Pp

passionately *adverb* full of passion or strong feeling

peacefully *adverb* quietly and calmly

peek *verb* to look quickly whilst partly visible, as if hiding behind something

peril *noun* serious danger or risk

pest *noun* something that is annoying or causes damage

plough (UK spelling)/**plow** (US spelling) *noun* a large farming tool used to turn the soil over

pollinate *verb* to move pollen to a plant to help the plant make seeds

Rr

reject *verb* refuse to accept someone or something

report *noun* an account of something that has happened

roots *noun* a person's family or cultural background

Ss

scent *verb* smell

scold *verb* blame someone crossly

scrumptious *adjective* delicious

season *noun* one of the four periods of the year: spring, summer, autumn and winter

shake *verb* move something about quickly

shape poem *noun* a poem in which the words are arranged in a special shape

sheer *adjective* extremely steep or vertical

sibling *noun* a brother or sister

signal *noun* a sign

skeleton *noun* the framework of bones that supports or contains an animal's body

snooty *adjective* showing disapproval towards others, especially those considered to belong to a lower social class

snuggle *verb* get comfortable or cuddle up

species *noun* a group of living things that are similar and can produce young together

spin *verb* turn round and round quickly

stitch *verb* sew with thread

sturdiness *noun* strength and solidity

supply *noun* something that is kept and is ready to be used when it is needed

surface *noun* the top or outside part of something

syllable *noun* a word or part of a word with one vowel sound

Tt

tentatively *adverb* hesitantly or uncertainly

toil *verb* work hard

tradition *noun* something that people have done the same way for a very long time

tumble *verb* fall

Uu

unique *adjective* one of a kind

unmistakable *adjective* not likely to be mistaken for something or someone else

Vv

vale *noun* a poetic word for a valley

valley *noun* low land between hills or mountains

Ww

waste *verb* use something carelessly

waterproof *adjective* made of a material that does not let water through it

well *noun* a deep hole in the ground from which you can get water

whoosh *verb* make a rushing sound

wrench *verb* pull or twist something suddenly

200 High frequency words

A

across
after
again
air
along
am
animals
another
any
around
away

B

baby
bad
bear
because
bed
been
before
began
best

better
birds
boat
book
box
boy

C

can't
car
cat
clothes
cold
coming
couldn't
cried

D

dark
did
didn't
different
dog
door

dragon
duck

E

each
eat
eggs
end
even
ever
every
everyone
eyes

F

fast
feet
fell
find
first
fish
floppy
fly
food

found
fox
friends
fun

G

garden
gave
giant
girl
going
gone
good
gran
grandad
great
green
grow

H

hard
has
hat
head

he's
home
horse
hot
how

I

I'll
inside
its
I've

J

jumped

K

keep
key
king
know

L

last
laughed
let

let's

liked

live

lived

long

looking

looks

lots

M

_____

_____

_____

_____

_____

_____

_____

_____

N

narrator

need

never

new

next

night

O

once

only

or

other

our

over

P

park

place

plants

play

please

pulled

Q

queen

R

rabbit

ran

really

red

right

river

room

round

run

S

_____

_____

_____

_____

_____

_____

_____

_____

_____

T

take

tea

tell

than

that's

there's

these

thing

things

think

thought

three

through

told

took

top

town

tree

trees

two

U

under

us

use

W

_____

_____

_____

_____

_____

_____

Y

yes

A Here are all the high frequency words that begin with the letter M. Add them in the correct place to the list on page 63, putting them in alphabetical order.

more   man   must   mouse   may   many   magic

much   mother   morning   miss   most

B Here are all the high frequency words that begin with the letter S. Add them in the correct place to the list on page 63, putting them in alphabetical order.

school   shouted   stop   sea   something

still   soon   small   suddenly   sat

sleep   snow   sun   stopped   say

C Here are all the high frequency words that begin with the letter W. Add them in the correct place to the list on page 63, putting them in alphabetical order.

water   want   where   would   who

wanted   well   way   work   why   window

which   wind   wish   white   we're

A Find words from the list of high frequency words to put in the following boxes. Some words can go in more than one box.

nouns	adjectives	prepositions

adverbs	past verbs	present verbs

irregular verbs	question words

B In the list of high frequency words find five words that can be used both as a noun and a verb. Make two different sentences to show the different meanings.

Example: book

He **booked** a hotel for two nights.

He really enjoyed reading the adventure **book**.

_____

_____

_____

_____

_____

C Write a homophone, a word which sounds the same but is spelled differently, for the following words from the high frequency list. *Example*: red/read

sun _____   right _____

night _____   know _____

two _____   been _____

bear _____   our _____

You might need a dictionary to help you with these two.

or _____   horse _____

New Word List

Home language(s)	English

New Word List

Home language(s)	English

New Word List

Home language(s)	English

New Word List

Home language(s)	English

Great Clarendon Street, Oxford OX2 6DP

Oxford University Press is a department of the University of Oxford.
It furthers the University's objective of excellence in research, scholarship,
and education by publishing worldwide in

Oxford New York

Auckland   Cape Town   Dar es Salaam   Hong Kong   Karachi
Kuala Lumpur   Madrid   Melbourne   Mexico City   Nairobi
New Delhi   Shanghai   Taipei   Toronto

With offices in

Argentina   Austria   Brazil   Chile   Czech Republic   France   Greece
Guatemala   Hungary   Italy   Japan   Poland   Portugal   Singapore
South Korea   Switzerland   Thailand   Turkey   Ukraine   Vietnam

© Oxford University Press 2013

The moral rights of the authors have been asserted

Database right Oxford University Press (maker)

First published 2013

British Library Cataloguing in Publication Data

Data available

ISBN- 978-019-839035-0

20

Printed in China by Shanghai Offset Printing Products Ltd

Paper used in the production of this book is a natural, recyclable product made from wood grown in
sustainable forests. The manufacturing process conforms to the environmental regulations of the country
of origin.

Acknowledgements
The publisher and authors would like to thank the following for permission to use photographs and copyright
material:

p2: tovovan/Shutterstock; p5 top: Hywit Dimyadi/Shutterstock; p6 top: JL-art/Shutterstock; p6 centre:
pichayasri/Shutterstock; p6 bottom: casejustin/Shutterstock; p8: Gokcegoksel/Dreamstime; p9: korinoxe/
Shutterstock; p10: Julien Tromeur/Shutterstock; p11: lineartestpilot/Shutterstock; p12: mexrix/Shutterstock;
p14: ecco/Shutterstock; p15: shooarts/Shutterstock; p16: Schmeiser/Shutterstock; p17: agrino/Shutterstock;
p18: Bennyartist/Shutterstock; p20: laola/Shutterstock; p21: Dudi/Shutterstock; p22 top: kirbyedy/Shutterstock;
p22 bottom: Volhah/Shutterstock; p23: Christos Georghiou/Shutterstock; p24: Azuzl/Shutterstock; p26 top:
STILLFX/Shutterstock; p26 bottom: JoeFotoSS/Shutterstock; p27: Natykach Nataliia/Shutterstock; p28: Barry
Barnes/Shutterstock; p29: tujuh17belas/Shutterstock; p33: Alan Uster/Shutterstock; p34: sabri deniz kizil/
Shutterstock; p35: Kjpargeter/Shutterstock; p36 top: The Blue Planet/Shutterstock; p36 bottom: Lindybug/
Shutterstock; p38: olillia/Shutterstock; p41: Lorelyn Medina/Shutterstock; p42 bottom: mexrix/Shutterstock;
p44, p45: Thanamat Somwan/Shutterstock; p47: Natalia Lavrinenko/Shutterstock; p48: jannoon028/Shutterstock;
p50: Kjpargeter/Shutterstock; p51 left: John T Takai/Shutterstock; p51 right: vectorOK/Shutterstock;
p52: Matthew Cole/Shutterstock; p53: Lorelyn Medina/Shutterstock; p54 top: Nate Widick/Shutterstock;
p54 bottom: Mariya Lebedinskaya/Shutterstock.

Cover illustration: Andy Elkerton

Illustrations are by: Mark Beech, Patricia Castelao, Milena Jahier, Marcin Piwowarski, Iva Sasheva

The author and publisher are grateful for permission to reprint extracts from the following copyright material:

Catherine and Laurence Anholt: 'My Sister Lives in Singapore' from *Big Book of Families* (Walker Books, 2000),
copyright © Catherine and Laurence Anholt 1998, reprinted by permission of Walker Books Ltd, London SE11
5HJ, www.walker.co.uk.

Brian Patten: 'The Tree and the Pool' from *Gargling with Jelly* (Viking, 2003) copyright © Brian Patten1985,
reprinted by permission of Penguin Books Ltd and the author c/o Rogers Coleridge & White, 20 Powis Mews,
London W11 1JN.

Any third party use of this material, outside of this publication, is prohibited. Interested parties should apply
to the copyright holders indicated in each case.

Although we have made every effort to trace and contact all copyright holders before publication this has not
been possible in all cases. If notified, the publisher will rectify any errors or omissions at the earliest
opportunity.

Oxford International English 4

Oxford International English is a structured course that delivers reading comprehension, writing and speaking and listening skills to students aged 5-11. Theme based units of fiction, non-fiction and poetry from around the world motivate students who have English as a first language or additional language.

This Workbook:

▸ Provides additional material based on the Student Books

▸ Includes student-friendly self-assessment activities for each unit so students feel confident in their learning

▸ Contains a dictionary section giving definitions of all the words from the Word Clouds and new word lists

▸ Is ideal for independent self-study and homework

Also available:

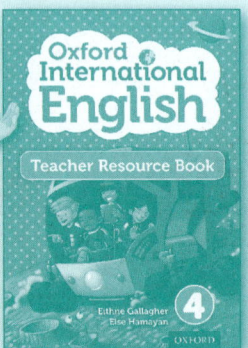
9780198390367

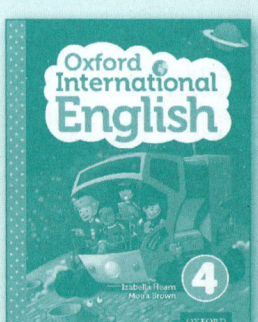
9780198390343

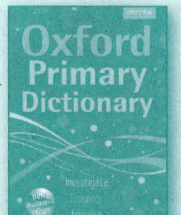
9780192732637

Other levels available   ⑥

OXFORD
UNIVERSITY PRESS

How to get in contact:
web   www.oxfordprimary.co.uk/ie
email   schools.enquiries.uk@oup.com
tel   +44 (0)1536 452610
fax   +44 (0)1865 313472

ISBN 978-0-19-839035-0

9 780198 390350